25
Powerful Prayers to Take You To Great Faith

"Designed by jcomp / Freepik"

Yolanda Washington-Cowan

Unless otherwise indicated, scriptures are taken from the New King James Version (NKJV).

25 Powerful Prayers To Take You To Great Faith
Copyright @ 2019

ISBN-13:978-0-9997776-6-4
ISBN-10: 0-9997776-6-1

by Yolanda Washington-Cowan
All rights reserved.
Published by
B-Inspired Publishing
7285 Winchester Road, Suite 109
Memphis, TN 38125
www.B-Inspiredpub.com
Printed in the United States
First Edition: March 2018

All rights reserved under International Copyright Law. Contents and/or cover may not be reproduced in whole or in part in any form without the expressed written consent of the Publisher.

Table of Contents

INTRODUCTION 1
PRAYER ONE.. 5
PRAYER TWO.. 8
PRAYER THREE 10
PRAYER FOUR 12
PRAYER FIVE... 13
PRAYER SIX 16
PRAYER SEVEN 17
PRAYER EIGHT.. 19
PRAYER NINE 22
PRAYER TEN 23
PRAYER ELEVEN 25
PRAYER TWELVE 28
PRAYER THIRTEEN 30
PRAYER FOURTEEN 32
PRAYER FIFTEEN.. 35
PRAYER SIXTEEN 37
PRAYER SEVENTEEN 40
PRAYER EIGHTEEN 42

PRAYER NINETEEN 44
PRAYER TWENTY 46
PRAYER TWENTY-ONE 48
PRAYER TWENTY-TWO 52
PRAYER TWENTY-THREE 52
PRAYER TWENTY-FOUR 54
PRAYER TWENTY-FIVE 55

INTRODUCTION

A few years ago, my son was diagnosed with Crohn's disease, and this shocking revelation nearly threw me off balance. As my son was fighting this disease, I witnessed his weight going from 225 to 145. Several doctors' visits seemed like there was never going to be an end to testing, and his body was rejecting all types of food. But I refused to accept the medical diagnosis because I was convinced that this illness was not my son's reality in Christ. So, my son and I began to speak healing over his life. Afterwards, we sang and praised God in advance;we were confident that God had answered our prayers. I remembered what the scripture said, that the prayers of the righteous availed much. I focused on it, and it worked for me. Today, my son is totally free from Crohn's. No trace of any known or unknown ailment in his body.

As believers, our reality in Christ Jesus is established by our faith in God. Whenever we are going through difficult times, we should always remember and believe God's promises for our lives according to the scriptures. The paths across life are not always smooth and straight. But God has assured us of His care and love if we can trust and have faith in Him. Faith is a powerful spiritual tool to unlock closed doors of healing, abundance, deliverance, fruitfulness, and favor. The scripture according to Romans 10:17 says, "So then faith cometh by hearing, and hearing by the word of God."

I believe that these 25 prayers will tremendously boost your faith in God. As you pray with an open mind, you will experience a dramatic increase in your faith and begin to access every blessing God has designed for your life.

Prayer Requests:_____

PRAYER ONE

These things I have written to you who believe in the name of the Son of God, that you may know that you have eternal life, and that you may continue to believe in the name of the Son of God. I John 5:13

Dear Father,

Thank you for the abundant life I have in you through Christ Jesus. I've done nothing to deserve the love that you show me. You saved me even while I was living in sin. Your mercy, love, and compassion rescued me from the punishment of my iniquities. You sacrificed Jesus Christ on the Cross of Calvary so that my sins could be washed away. You transitoned me from the realm of darkness, cluelessness, and ignorance to the kingdom of light, understanding, and knowledge of your perfect will for me through Your Son, Christ Jesus. I wasn't saved by my own work. I was saved by your grace.

Sweet Father, there's nothing I can do to repay your sacrifices other than to continue to believe in the name of Jesus Christ. Lord Jesus, I have great faith in your mighty power and your saving grace that has qualified me to be a partaker of your priceless salvation. I have no doubt that you will continue to guide me through life and strengthen me to overcome more challenges, tribulations, and persecutions.

Thank you, Lord Jesus. Amen

Prayer

*Requests:*_____

_____

_____

_____

_____

_____

_____

_____

_____

_____

PRAYER TWO

But the Scripture has confined all under sin, that the promise by faith in Jesus Christ might be given to those who believe. Galatians 3:22

My heavenly Father,

I appreciate you for all the spiritual blessings you have made available to me through Christ Jesus. Although I sometimes get so carried away by life situations that I forget about your awesome promises for my life, but today, Lord I have come to say that I am sorry for those times I failed to believe in your Word. I am sorry for those moments I had to put my hope in humans. For those days, I doubted your ability to grant my heart's desires. Lord, I am sorry.

Reading through your Word in the Scriptures has revealed to me the power and benefits of trusting you. Today, I stop relying on my ability, wisdom, and connections. I tap into your inexhaustible grace by faith. I surrender everything to you. I believe it is only in you that my life can be made complete. I receive everlasting life, divine provision, healing, wisdom, sound mind, and good success by faith in the name of Jesus Christ.

Amen!

Prayer Requests:_____
_____
_____
_____
_____
_____
_____
_____
_____
_____
_____
_____
_____
_____
_____

PRAYER THREE

I have been crucified with Christ; it is no longer I who live, but Christ lives in me; and the life which I now live in the flesh I live by faith in the Son of God, who loved me and gave Himself for me.
Galatians 2:20

I am inseparable from Christ Jesus, my Savior. His reality is my reality. I am what He says I am. I live by faith in the Son of God who loved and died for my sins; who paid a supreme sacrifice so that I might live. His work of redemption was aimed at saving me from the curse of law and sin. Jesus Christ rendered death powerless when He rose up three days later after He had liberated the tormented and freed the oppressed. Jesus triumphed over death and sin; I believe I have received power and grace to overcome every difficult life situation.

By faith, I celebrate my victory over untimely death, sin, and iniquities. I live a holy life approved by God. I have dominion in Christ Jesus. I am exempted from shame, poverty, failure, sickness, and disease in Jesus' name. I bask in God's unending love. I am totally free from sin because Christ has paid the price.

Hallelujah!

Prayer

Requests: _____

_____
_____
_____
_____
_____
_____
_____
_____
_____
_____
_____

PRAYER FOUR

But let him ask in faith, with no doubting, for he who doubts is like a wave of the sea driven and tossed by the wind. For let not that man suppose that he will receive anything from the Lord; he is a double-minded man, unstable in all his ways.
James 1: 6-8

Lord Jesus,

Today, I receive the grace to have undying faith in your promises for my life. Your Word has taught me that it is by my faith that I can have an answer to my prayers. I completely believe your Word for my life. Your Word of peace comforts me in the time of trouble. I find meaning in this disorganized world. My life begins to take a new course of spiritual growth and financial progression in the name of Jesus. I receive all spiritual blessings that you've assigned to my life from the beginning of time.

Nothing comes in-between me and my miracles because I believe in God who is the Almighty. My health is enriched; my finances are blessed; and my soul is preserved to witness more amazing days, weeks, months, and years of my life. I gain stability in my faith in God. Nothing hinders me from fully leaning on the Lord. Thank you Lord, Jesus. Amen

Prayer Requests: _____

PRAYER FIVE

But as many as received Him, to them He gave the right to become children of God, to those who believe in His name. John 1:12

I declare that I am of the Lord, born of God and designed to do exploits in this world. Even if my current situation is nothing to write home about, my reality is in Christ Jesus the One who died for my sins and rose on the third day. I'm free from every bondage of sin and iniquity. Every power and principality limiting my freedom is neutralized by the Lord Jesus. I live in dominion. Your Word says that whoever is freed by the Father such is free indeed.

I receive the life of God and reflect His glory everywhere I go. I receive a sound mind to hope, to believe, and to trust in the Lord. I am a child of God. I am born again. I am entitled to every spiritual blessing in my Father's kingdom. I live in the splendor of His glory. I bring men to the light of the salvation of God. I am a living testimony of God's faithfulness. I am garbed in His garment of holiness. His grace abides with me forever. Amen

Prayer Requests: _____

_____
_____
_____
_____
_____
_____
_____
_____
_____
_____
_____
_____
_____
_____
_____

PRAYER SIX

He who believes in Him is not condemned; but he who does not believe is condemned already because he has not believed in the name of the only begotten Son of God. John 3:18

Jesus, the Son of God, I believe in you. You came to this sinful world and died for my sins. My iniquities and shortcomings, you took away. With your precious blood, you redeemed me, saved me, and freed me from the sting of death. Today, I accept your reign and renew my commitment to follow you faithfully in my life. I am not ignorant of the sacrifices you made to qualify me as a joint-heir in the kingdom of God. Bless you Lord.

I am not condemned because I have accepted your life. I am no longer a slave to sin. I have power over the forces of darkness. I live in victory. The new life I have in you, guarantees my access to supernatural blessings. I am rich in wisdom, foresight, and insight. I am not oblivious to the schemes of the devil. The devil is rendered powerless at the sight of your presence in my life. I have the mark of Christ everywhere I go. I cannot be accused of any former wrongs because Jesus is now in control of my life.

I believe I am forever saved in Christ Jesus. Amen!

Prayer

Requests_____

_____
_____
_____
_____
_____
_____
_____
_____
_____
_____
_____
_____
_____
_____

PRAYER SEVEN

Resist him, steadfast in the faith, knowing that the same sufferings are experienced by your brotherhood in the world. I Peter 5:9

I submit myself to You Lord. I rebuke and resist the devil. I refuse to listen or subscribe to the doubting spirit in me asking if you are truly able to help me in this difficult time. I give up on my ability to bring all my heart desires to reality. Now, more than ever, I realize that you have answers to all the questions I have been asking. You answer prayers in your own time. So, there is no point bothering myself over the things that only you can do. I believe that you are never late. You are always on time. You do what no one else can do. You are the Almighty.

I believe all my trials, failures, difficulties, and disappointments are but for a while. You are the solution, and you are on the way already. I know that I am going through this situation for a reason. I am not bothered by what people say about me. I am not worried about my present condition anymore. I put all my burdens on you. I receive rest, peace of mind, and satisfaction from you, Lord Jesus. It is well with my soul. I rejoice!

Prayer

Requests_____

_____

_____

_____

_____

_____

_____

_____

_____

_____

_____

_____

_____

_____

PRAYER EIGHT

And Jesus said to them, "I am the bread of life. He who comes to Me shall never hunger, and he who believes in Me shall never thirst. But I said to you that you have seen Me and yet do not believe. All that the Father gives Me will come to Me, and the one who comes to Me I will by no means cast out.
John 6:35-37

Dear Great Provider,

I put all my trust in you for my divine protection and provision. Today, I make a decision to stop prioritizing my wisdom and intellect over what your grace can give me. I have languished for long to seek comfort and peace. But the more I tried, the more frustrated I became. I look on to you this day with the plainness of heart and complete trust. My faith in you is rekindled. I believe that I have access to every good gift in your kingdom.

Christ Jesus, your Word says whoever comes to you will not be cast out. Lord, I believe my petitions before you will not be discarded. I have the assurance that the end has come to my disapointtments and frustrations. I begin to take charge of the situation. I walk in power. I walk in glory. I live a life of favor as of today. I dwell in your kingdom forever. Amen

Prayer Requests_____

_____

_____

_____

_____

_____

_____

_____

_____

_____

_____

_____

_____

_____

_____

PRAYER NINE

Therefore, I say to you, whatever thing you ask when you pray, believe that you receive them, and you will have them. Mark 11:24

Dear Redeemer,

I thank you, my heavenly Father because I have the assurance that I will receive whatever I ask for in my prayers today. I bless you for your faithfulness even from ages past. I cannot thank you enough for those great things you have done in the past in my life, family and among my friends. I am confident that you will not put me to shame this time around. Because you are the same yesterday, today and forever.

Today, I pray and receive grace to excel and make an impact in my world. I am unstoppable in my career and business. My marriage receives your unending blessings. I am highly favored wherever I go. The unconditional mercy of God locates me this day. I am blessed, and I bless others too. I have the knowledge of the Word of God, and I rejoice knowing that Christ died for me and washed all my sins away. I declare and decree that difficulty is not my portion anymore. I now live a purpose-driven life. I am no longer confused. I am bold, confident, and wise. I possess all my possessions in Christ Jesus. Amen!

Prayer

Requests:_____

_____
_____
_____
_____
_____
_____
_____
_____
_____
_____
_____
_____
_____
_____

PRAYER TEN

Jesus said to her, "Did I not say to you that if you would believe you would see the glory of God?"
John 11:40

Christ Jesus, I am sorry to have ever doubted you in the past. Now, I can see that you are a faithful God. You are not a man that you should lie. You place greater importance on your Word more than your names. Your Word of hope is my strength. Your faithfulness is my conviction of your ability to save me and grant me all my heart's desires.

You know my expectations. Everything about me, you know. Your Word says that you knew me even before I was formed in my mother's womb. Therefore, I believe you have the perfect solution for my life. I am tired of trying to help you. It's your case, and I believe you are handling it already. I rely on your Word that says we shall have anything that we ask for in prayer if we believe that you can do it. I believe you can do exceedingly, abundantly more than what I ask for or desire. I believe you have perfected that which concerns me. Glory be to your name in the highest! Thank you Lord. Amen!

Prayer Requests: _____

_____

_____

_____

_____

_____

_____

_____

_____

_____

_____

_____

_____

PRAYER ELEVEN

For with God nothing will be impossible. Luke 1:37

God, the Almighty, the most gracious, the most merciful. You are the God of all flesh, and there is nothing impossible for you to do. You parted the sea and made the children of Israel walk on the dry land while the battalions of Egypt were consumed in the sea. Your Word healed the sick, freed the oppressed, and delivered the bound. By your power, you do great, amazing, improbable things impossible for humans. You are the only awesome God.

Undoubtedly, you have proven countless times to us in the Scriptures that you are reliable and dependable. You never fail your own people. Even in our unrighteousness, you have shown that you love us. You go out of your way for us. You don't judge us by our own holiness or righteousness before you give us our heart's desires. Dear Father, today, I realize there is nothing more logical, nothing more reasonable and nothing wiser I could do at this time than to follow you wholeheartedly and believe your Word. For all my requests, I believe you have granted them. I begin to enjoy the ever-flowing grace of God in my life, in my marriage, and in my career in Jesus' name. Amen!

Prayer Requests: _____

_____
_____
_____
_____
_____
_____
_____
_____
_____
_____
_____
_____
_____
_____
_____

PRAYER TWELVE

But what does it say? "The your Word is near you, in your mouth and in your heart" (that is, the your Word of faith which we preach): that if you confess with your mouth the Lord Jesus and believe in your heart that God has raised Him from the dead, you will be saved. Romans 10:9

God of righteousness,

I have no reservation about the miraculous work of redemption that you sent Jesus Christ to do for me and the entire human race. It was a huge sacrifice to have your only begotten Son slaughtered so that others would live. I have no doubt that Jesus has perfected my salvation on the Cross and has caused me to be a partaker in your glorious kingdom. I am a chosen generation, called forth to show your excellence across the length and breadth of the universe. I am saved by faith, and I labor to bring more people to the light of what you have done for them through Christ Jesus, my Savior.

Blessed Father, I believe I receive divine support to remain in your presence throughout my lifetime. I receive the grace to follow diligently and welcome each change you bring across to my life. I reflect the love of Christ to everyone around me. It is well with my body, my spirit, and my soul in Jesus' precious name. Amen!

Prayer Requests: _____
_____
_____
_____
_____
_____
_____
_____
_____
_____
_____
_____
_____
_____
_____
_____

PRAYER THIRTEEN

For with the heart one believes unto righteousness, and with the mouth confession is made unto salvation. For the Scripture says, "Whoever believes on Him will not be put to shame."
Romans 10:10

*D*ear Gracious Father,
I thank you Jesus for the salvation of my soul. I am glad because I am no longer a captive of the devil and sin. Your precious bloodshed on the Cross justified me. You called me to be part of your everlasting kingdom. You washed me in your blood, and now I am as holy as my Father in heaven.

I am a believer. I don't subscribe or submit to the craftiness of the devil and his agents. I live a holy life approved by God. My mind is conditioned to meditate on God's Your Word daily without ceasing. I have dominion in Christ. I live in dominion. I bring more men and women to the light of God.

I have everything I need through Jesus Christ. I don't lack any good thing. My God is faithful with His Your Word to supply all my needs according to His riches in glory. Poverty is not my portion. I live in the affluence and splendor of our heavenly Father.

I am forever blessed! In Jesus name, Amen!

Prayer Requests:_____

_____
_____
_____
_____
_____
_____
_____
_____
_____
_____
_____
_____
_____
_____
_____
_____
_____

PRAYER FOURTEEN

So Jesus said to them, "Because of your unbelief, for assuredly, I say to you, if you have faith as a mustard seed, you will say to this mountain, 'Move from here to there,' and it will move; and nothing will be impossible for you. However, this kind does not go out except by prayer and fasting."
Matthew 17:20

Dear Christ Jesus,

Thank you Lord for the knowledge of what faith in you can do. It's so amazing that you are not even asking for much. You only want me to align my expectations to your purpose for my life. Before now, I was guilty of disbelief. But today, I am relieved because I have found a new life of ease and comfort in you. My new life came as a result of my encounter with you.

As I continue in my journey of faith, I receive the grace to always trust and follow you even in stressful situations. I refuse to give expression to my fear and doubt. My faith is increased in you. I excel in everything I lay my hands on. I receive all the blessings you have designed for me through Christ Jesus. Amen.

Prayer Requests:

PRAYER FIFTEEN

That he would grant you, according to the riches of His glory, to be strengthened with might through His Spirit in the inner man, that Christ may dwell in your hearts through faith; that you, being rooted and grounded in love... Ephesians 3:16-17

*B*lessed Redeemer,
I believe you dwell in my heart because I am a firm believer in the death and resurrection of our Lord Jesus Christ. I receive strength for my heart today to consistently increase in faith in you. Through faith, I gain access to your inexhaustible glory. I bask in the excitement of my salvation. Not by my own power or might, but through your unconditional love.

I demonstrate the love of God everywhere I go. People see my light and get drawn to God. I live within the reality of eternity. I am led by the Spirit of God. I don't rely on my thinking. I receive direction and inspiration from the Almighty before embarking on any journey. I can never be tired of trusting in the Lord. My faith in the Lord is the fuel that powers my trajectory. Forever, I am rooted and grounded in the love of God. Amen!

Prayer Requests: _____

_____
_____
_____
_____
_____
_____
_____
_____
_____
_____
_____
_____
_____

PRAYER SIXTEEN

Then Jesus answered and said to her, "O woman, great is your faith! Let it be to you as you desire." And her daughter was healed from that very hour.
Matthew 15:8

Jesus Christ my helper,

Today, I turn to you and seek your support to boost my faith in you. I receive answers to all my open and secret prayers. I declare by faith that all my challenges, anxieties, and difficulties are over because I have you in my life. I don't care about individual opinions. I am not moved by people's disbelief. I lean solely on your promises. The Spirit of God strengthens me to pattern my life in alignment with your purpose for my life in Jesus' name.

I receive a bountiful harvest from my seed of faith. I shall not lack anything good because my heavenly is super rich in glory. I part ways with sickness and diseases. It's my season of supernatural healing and abundance. I claim and receive all God's promises for my life in Jesus' name. Amen

Prayer

Requests:_____

_____

_____

_____

_____

_____

_____

_____

_____

_____

_____

_____

_____

_____

PRAYER SEVENTEEN

Watch, stand fast in the faith, be brave, be strong. Let all that you do be done with love.
I Corinthians 16: 13-14

Today, I declare that nothing will cause me to doubt the love of God for my life – not sickness, not persecution, not disappointment, and not rejection. I have seen the light. The devil cannot deceive me any more. I live in the knowledge of what God has done for me. I could not save myself, but He did it for me. He clothed me with glory and restored peace to my mind. God took away my fear and replaced it with boldness.

I am not an ingrate. I stand strong and fast in the faith. I allow God to always take the lead in my decision and in the choices I make. I don't push my agenda first. I allow you, Lord, to have your way. I am no more in charge of my life. Christ is. Christ is what I live. I am forever joined with Him. I am of the Lord! Amen!

Prayer Requests:_____

_____
_____
_____
_____
_____
_____
_____
_____
_____
_____
_____
_____
_____
_____

PRAYER EIGHTEEN

But you, O man of God, flee these things and pursue righteousness, godliness, faith, love, patience, gentleness. Fight the good fight of faith, lay hold on eternal life, to which you were also called and have confessed the good confession in the presence of many witnesses. I Timothy 6:11-12

My Righteous Lord,

Today, I renew my commitment to pursue righteousness, godliness, faith, love, patience, gentleness, and all other spiritual qualities you desire to see in your children. I forsake the work of the flesh today. I embrace the eternal truth of the gospel and live righteously as desired by my heavenly Father. I renounce the devil and his works. I will do good things.

I repent from all my sins and iniquities. I believe I have received forgiveness from God. There is no condemnation for me ever again. I have the life of Christ in me. I do not struggle to please God. I have the mark of Christ in my body. I am a joint heir to God's kingdom. I partake in the blessings of the kingdom by your divine will. I am the elect of God. All things have become new in my life. The old nature is gone forever. I am saved!

Prayer

Requests:_____

_____
_____
_____
_____
_____
_____
_____
_____
_____
_____

PRAYER NINETEEN

He who believes in Me, as the scripture has said, out of his heart will flow rivers of living water.
John 7:38

Dear Lord Jesus, I believe in everything the Scripture has said about you. I believe that you died for my sins, and you rose on the third day. I believe that through your sacrifice, the wall of death and sin was crushed down. I believe that humanity received salvation through you. I believe you broke the curse of the law and that I now live under grace. But I also understand that your grace is not an expression of permission for us to indulge in sins and iniquities. I believe through faith, we have power and dominion over the devil and sin.

A river of living water flows out of my heart. Therefore, I reflect the light of God to the people around me. You healed the sick, raised the dead, and restored power to the feeble. So, I believe I have the same power. I declare healing to the sick, and I receive an instant result. I raise the dead by faith. I lead people to Christ. I believe!

Prayer Requests:_____

_____
_____
_____
_____
_____
_____
_____
_____
_____
_____
_____
_____
_____

PRAYER TWENTY

And my speech and my preaching were not with persuasive your Words of human wisdom, but in demonstration of the Spirit and of power, that your faith should not be in the wisdom of men but in power of God. I Corinthians 2:5

Today, I receive the grace to demonstrate great faith in God in every situation of my life. I will not position God to play second fiddle. I allow Him to guide and direct my path. I relegate my wisdom and exalt the Spirit and power of God to provide a solution in all situations. I live a life of faith. I rejoice in the supernatural provisions of God for my life. I leverage the grace of God on my life to unlock doors of good health, prosperity, foresight, inspiration, and creativity. I don't utter empty your Words. My utterances are backed by God's approval. I live just and right. I am blessed in Jesus' name. Amen!

Prayer

Requests:_____

_____
_____
_____
_____
_____
_____
_____
_____
_____
_____
_____
_____
_____
_____
_____

PRAYER TWENTY-ONE

Not that we have dominion over your faith, but are fellow workers for your joy; for by faith you stand.
II Corinthians 1:24

Dear Christ Jesus,

I ask and receive the grace to stand on your promises for my life. I refuse to yield to the temptation of leaning on my own understanding. I receive the wisdom of God to live in line with the divine purpose of God for me and my generation. The grace of God upholds me throughout the journey of my faith. The Lord shines his light on my path so that I will not go astray. Your guidance is the reason that I am winning the battles of life. Lord, in everything I do, I submit to your will. Thank you Lord, for you are my hope, my refuge, and strength. Nothing will derail me from the path of righteousness in Jesus' name. Amen!

Prayer

Requests:_____

_____

_____

_____

_____

_____

_____

_____

_____

_____

_____

_____

_____

PRAYER TWENTY–TWO

For by grace you have been saved through faith, and not of yourselves; it is the gift of God, not of works, lest anyone should boast. For we are His workmanship, created in Christ Jesus for good works, which God prepared beforehand that we should walk in them. Ephesians 2:8-10

Thank you Precious Savior for loving me. Your priceless blood washed my sins away and made me righteous. By faith, you saved me from the curse of the law and sin. You overpowered death and gave me everlasting life. I was not saved by my works or service in the church. My works aren't sufficient to rescue me from the grip of death and destruction. But your Blood did. You had compassion on me. You showed me your mercy. You vindicated me in the presence of my accusers. I live triumphantly knowing that you have overcome the world for me. I bask in the joy of the Holy Ghost.

Thank you for loving me. Blessed be unto your holy name. Amen

Prayer Requests:_____

PRAYER TWENTY-THREE

But that no one is justified by the law in the sight of God is evident, for "the just shall live by faith." Yet the law is not of faith, but "the man who does them shall live by them." Galatians 3:11-12

I live by faith. I have dominion by faith. I take kingdoms and territories by faith. I live righteously. I demonstrate the righteousness of God through my conduct and actions. God has forgiven me of all my sins and iniquities. There is no condemnation for me again. God has turned His eyes to me. He has favored me. He has blessed me. He has liberated me from every satanic entanglement. I am free from bondage.

Christ Jesus, I receive the grace to work without blame in your presence. By your grace, through faith, I totally suppress the influence of flesh in my life. I give the Holy Spirit of God expression in my life. He begins to direct and guide my footsteps. I am not confused. I have the light of God in me. Forever. I am God's! Amen!

Prayer Requests:_____

PRAYER TWENTY-FOUR

Looking unto Jesus, the author and finisher of our faith, who for the joy that was set before Him endured the cross, despising the shame, and has sat down at the right hand of the throne of God.
Hebrew 12:2

The scripture says if the Spirit that raised Jesus Christ from the dead lives in us, that same Spirit will quicken our mortal body. Lord, I receive by faith the Spirit of God that raised Jesus from the dead. I declare that my body is quickened.

I am free from harm, death, despair, frustration, failure, shame, and diseases because Jesus Christ had buried all my troubles on the cross. His resurrection resurged me. Now, I am living a new life, designed, approved, and sustained by God. It's well with me. Amen!

Prayer Requests: _____

_____
_____
_____
_____
_____
_____
_____
_____
_____
_____
_____
_____
_____
_____
_____

PRAYER TWENTY–FIVE

For God so loved the world that He gave His only begotten Son, that whoever believes in Him should not perish but have everlasting life. John 3:16

Lord, I receive the everlasting life of God because I believe in the death, burial, and resurrection of my dear Savior, Christ Jesus. Unlike Abel's blood that was crying for vengeance, the blood of Jesus washed me clean. I am now entitled to the heavenly gifts of divine provision, safety, security, and abundance in all ramifications.

No evil can move close to me because I carry in my body the mark of Christ. God has vindicated me from every charge levied against me. I have been discharged and acquitted from the satanic court. No one is permitted to trouble me again because I am born again. I live the life of Christ. I reflect Jesus Christ wherever I go. I am saved forever. Amen!

Prayer Requests:_____

_____
_____
_____
_____
_____
_____
_____
_____
_____
_____
_____
_____
_____

Beloved reader, I believe by praying these prayers, your faith life has been transformed. You have transitioned to great faith in our Lord Jesus Christ. Amen!

www.ingramcontent.com/pod-product-compliance
Lightning Source LLC
Chambersburg PA
CBHW020830020526
44118CB00032B/525